ALEKSANDR ORLOV

PRESENTS

SERGEI'S

SPACE ADVENTURE

MEERKAT CLASSICS
RUSSIA 2012

Sergei's Space Adventure
ALEKSANDR ORLOV

1 3 5 7 9 10 8 6 4 2

First published in 2012 by Ebury Press, an imprint of Ebury Publishing

A Random House Group company

Copyright © **compare**the**meerkat**.com 2012

comparethe**meerkat**.com has asserted its right to be identified as the author of this Work in accordance with the Copyright, Designs and Patents Act 1988

This is an advertisement feature on behalf of **compare**the**market**.com

comparethe**meerkat**.com and **compare**the**market**.com
are trading names of BISL Limited

The Random House Group Limited Reg. No. 954009

Addresses for companies within the Random House Group can be found at www.randomhouse.co.uk

A CIP catalogue record for this book is available from the British Library

The Random House Group Limited supports The Forest Stewardship Council (FSC®), the leading international forest certification organisation. Our books carrying the FSC label are printed on FSC® certified paper. FSC is the only forest certification scheme endorsed by the leading environmental organisations, including Greenpeace. Our paper procurement policy can be found at www.randomhouse.co.uk/environment

MIX
Paper from
responsible sources
FSC® C013123

Printed and bound in Italy by Graphicom SRL

ISBN 9780091949990

To buy books by your favourite authors and register for offers visit www.randomhouse.co.uk

This is a work of fiction. Names and characters are the product of the author's imagination and any resemblance to actual persons, living or dead, is entirely coincindental

A MESSAGE FROM THE AUTHOR

Please be seat for new exciting adventure.

Just for once we are letting Sergei take the limelights. (Who say I am not generous boss?)

As all peoples know, Sergei is now very old and moulty, and his tea tastes of sadness. He is sadness because of his worms, and also because he lose his job with the Mir(kat) Space Programme many year ago. (He was award medal for moon landing, which they take away when they find out he fake it up in his garage). Now he is always pine for days of space.

So this story – full of science and thrillsy suspense – is Sergei's day in the sunshine. He must make the most of it, as he is getting behind with his work and needs to get back to his computermabob.

Yours,

Aleksandr

ALEKSANDR ORLOV

Far from little village of Meerkovo, deep in heart of Russia, is a **secret space lab.** It is launch site of Mir(kat) space probe, and is where all the cleverest meerkats in the world make rockets that fly into space.

It is hidden by trees and mountains and is surround by electric anti-mongoose fence. (The great Meerkat–Mongoose Space Race has been bitter battle for many year. Stinky mongooses are always try to steal rocket secrets).

One Tuesday, not long ago, the cleverest meerkats in the world have just finish build the Mir(kat) Rocket Spaceship Mark 1.

It was stand on launch pad and look all new and shiny. It **was taller than Mongoose Mountain** (which is very tall indeed) and was full of machines and buttons and dials. It was the most beautiful rocket in the world (probables).

Now, if you look carefully, you can see a tiny lift crawl up the side of rocket. If you look even more careful, you can see three figures in orange space suits standing inside.

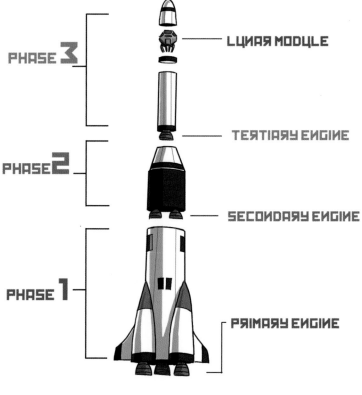

PHASE 3

LUNAR MODULE

TERTIARY ENGINE

PHASE 2

SECONDARY ENGINE

PHASE 1

PRIMARY ENGINE

SSP ROCKET ALPHA-T04

And if you look really, really careful you can see that one of them was **small and grey** and looked just like –

Sergei!

When he was a little grey meerpup (Sergei has been grey for as long as he can remember) Sergei went to space school. He learnt all about rockets and what made them fly.

Aeronautics, ballistics, combustions —
they were all as simples as ABC to little Sergei.

As he walk into rocket cabin, Sergei see that one of the seats had **Captain Sergei** sewn on to it. Breathless with excite, Sergei strap himself in.

Don't these straps look puzzley?
Clever Sergei for knowing how to undo!

"Three.

Two.

One.

We have lift!"

came the voice through his helmet.
With a whoooooosh that make all the blood rush
to Sergei's head, the rocket shot up into the air.

Sergei felt a little bit sick.

But then he see on screen in front of him the Mir(kat) Control Room. All the meerkat scientists were cheering and waving in delightedness. Sergei felt much better. Excited, he took off his straps and felt himself float up to the ceiling.

Then he saw a bag of beetle bits.*
They looked very invitings.

*Sergei has weakness for beetle bits.
Personally I find they go straight to the hind.

But when he opened the packet they go **floating all over cabin**, because they are weightlessness, just like Sergei. It was very difficult to catch all the beetle bits, but Sergei managed it.

Feeling rather full, Sergei turned a little green underneath his grey when the rocket start to jolt and shudder.*

*Sergei's is not strong stomach.
He has always had lots of quease.

But then with another bang and a wobble it came to complete stop. Sergei find himself floating towards the door just as it slowly open.

There in front of him was stony landscape.
It look just like beach without the sea. It was the moon!

Scarcely able to believe his eyes

(his spectacles had gone all misty inside his helmet), Sergei
stepped out and on to the moon.

"One giant leap for a meerkat, one small step for meerkind,"
said Sergei out loud, getting his words a bit mixed up.

See how deep is bootprint.
I think someone was trying to make big impression!

He reach behind him into the Mir(kat) Flag Compartment, and carefully lift out a Mir(kat) Flag. Waving it in triumphant (very slowly because of the weightlessness) he stuck it in the moon sand. Just as he was thinking of trying out the Moon Golf Clubs and Moon Golf Balls a voice boom in his helmet.

"Sergei."

It was not the Control Room of Mir(kat) HQ. It was...

... the dulcet tones... of... me! Aleksandr Orlov!

"Oh dear," thought Sergei.

He took off his helmet, wiped his spectacles and saw he was stand by the door of the computermabob room. And Mr Aleksandr was call him from his office. Perhaps his medication make him dream. **But in his paw was a small rock,** just like the ones on the moon. Sergei knew at that moment that he **HAD** been on the moon, and nobody and nothing could take that away from him.

Moon rock is full of hole.
Like piece of cheese, but not so tasty.

Aleksandr's Life Lesson

Never stop hoping for impossible,
even if you are Sergei.

Now read my other greatest tales

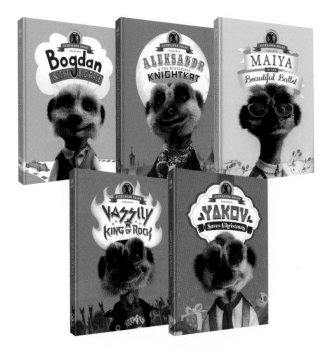

Available from all good bookshops

Also available to download as an ebookamabob
or audiomajig as read by the author – me!

For more information visit www.comparethemeerkat.com

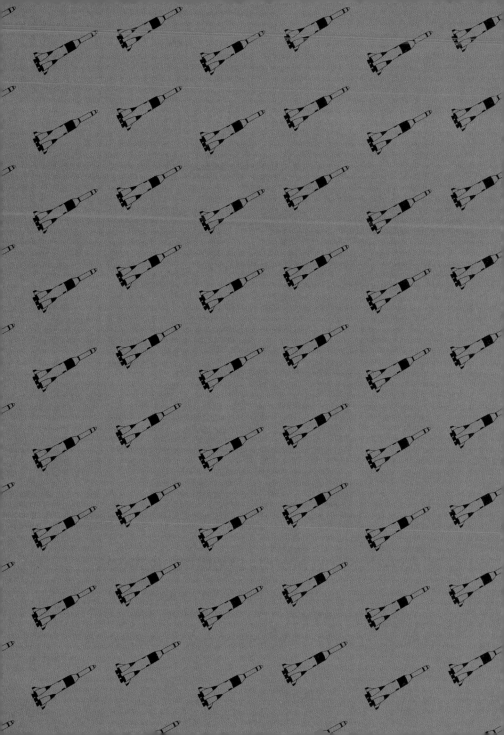